■ WAR VEHICLES ■

VEHICLES of the CIVIL WAR

by Pete Delmar

Consultant:
Dennis P. Mroczkowski
Colonel, U.S. Marine Corps Reserve (Retired)
Williamsburg, Virginia

CAPSTONE PRESS
a capstone imprint

Edge Books are published by Capstone Press,
1710 Roe Crest Drive, North Mankato, Minnesota 56003
www.capstonepub.com

Library of Congress Cataloging-in-Publication Data
Delmar, Pete.
Vehicles of the Civil War / by Pete Delmar.
pages cm.—(Edge books. War vehicles.)
Includes bibliographical references and index.
Summary: "Describes various land, air, and sea vehicles used by Union and
Confederate forces during the American Civil War"—Provided by publisher.
Audience: Grades 4-6.
ISBN 978-1-4296-9912-9 (library binding)
ISBN 978-1-4765-3377-3 (ebook PDF)
1. United States—History—Civil War, 1861–1865—Transportation—Juvenile literature.
2. Vehicles, Military—United States—History—19th century—Juvenile literature. 3.
Warships—United States—History—19th century—Juvenile literature. I. Title.
E491.D45 2014
973.7'3—dc23   2013004801

Editorial Credits
Aaron Sautter, editor; Heidi Thompson, designer; Eric Manske, production specialist

Photo Credits
Alamy: Everett Collection Inc, 16 (top), imagebroker, 18 (bottom), Niday Picture
Library, 7, 16b, North Wind Picture Archives, 17b; Corbis, 11 (both), 15b, 20 (both),
21, Bettmann, 4, 9 (both), 10b, 15t, 19, Medford Historical Society Collection, 10t, 12t,
23t; Getty Images: Archive Photos/Kean Collection, 17t, Archive Photos/Timothy H.
O'Sullivan, 8, Buyenlarge, 22t, MPI, 18t, Stock Montage, 9 (middle), Wood & Gibson/
George Eastman, 13t; James P. Rowan, 12b, 25t; Library of Congress, 13b, 14t; Mary
Evans Picture Library, 24t; National Archives and Records Administration, cover, 23b,
26, 27, 28, 29; SuperStock: imagebroker.net/H-D Falkenstein/ima, 14b; U.S. Naval
Historical Center, 25b; U.S. Navy illustration, 24b; Wikimedia, 22b

Artistic Effects
Shutterstock

Printed in the United States of America in Stevens Point, Wisconsin.
032013   007227WZF13

Table of Contents

Ch.1 > America's Civil War

The morning of July 1, 1863, began quietly in Gettysburg, Pennsylvania. But the sounds of battle soon surrounded the small town. For three days, screams mingled with explosions as cannon fire smashed army lines and supply wagons. The Battle of Gettysburg was one of the bloodiest of the Civil War (1861–1865). But it was an important turning point for the Union.

Both Union and Confederate armies relied on a variety of land vehicles during the war.

The Civil War was fought over slavery and states' rights. In the northern states, people often worked in factories and were paid for their work. But African-American slaves did much of the work in southern states. Slaves were forced to grow tobacco, cotton, and other crops for wealthy landowners.

Many northerners felt that slavery had to be stopped at any cost. President Abraham Lincoln also believed slavery was wrong and needed to come to an end. But people in the South weren't willing to give up their slaves. They believed that states had the right to decide for themselves about slavery and other issues.

In 1861 several southern states **seceded** from the Union. They formed their own country called the Confederate States of America. They created their own **constitution** and elected Jefferson Davis as their president. In response, President Lincoln made the difficult decision to go to war to end slavery and to keep the United States together as a single nation.

secede—to formally withdraw from a group or an organization, often to form another organization

constitution—the system of laws that states the rights of the people and the powers of the government

THE FIRST MODERN WAR

The Civil War is often called the first modern war. It took place during a time of great change and progress in technology. The Civil War was the first time armies used such a wide range of vehicles. Troops no longer just marched or rode horses to battlefields. They were carried by armored trains, wagons, and steamships.

Armored vehicles were used for the first time in combat. Tough ironclad ships began making a major difference in naval battles. Train cars were covered in armor and mounted with weapons for the first time. The Civil War also saw the first widespread use of rifled **artillery**, submarines, and gas-filled balloons during wartime.

The Union had a huge advantage in producing weapons and vehicles. The North's many factories and shipyards helped fuel the war effort. But the South's main focus had been on farms and growing crops. This difference in technology helped lead to the Confederates' defeat in 1865.

The Union used armored ships to attack and capture Fort Henry in Tennessee on February 6, 1862.

artillery—cannons and other large guns used during battles

Both the North and the South used a wide range of ground vehicles. Wagons of all kinds supported the war effort for both sides. Trains carried thousands of troops and tons of supplies. But perhaps the most important "vehicles" of all were the four-legged type.

···HORSES AND MULES···

Northern Horses

When the war broke out, the Union had about 3.4 million horses. Northern horses were used mainly for pulling carriages and wagons or for plowing fields. These horses were strong, reliable animals. But most of them could not match the speed of southern-bred horses.

WAR FACT

The war took a great toll on horses and mules. Armies rarely tried to save sick or wounded animals. They were often shot to end their suffering. About 1.5 million horses and mules died during the war.

Southern Horses

The Confederacy had only about 1.7 million horses. However, horse racing had long been a popular sport in the South. Most southern horses were bred to be fast runners and to have great endurance. These qualities made the horses perfect choices for use on the battlefield.

Horses and Mules in War

In both Union and Confederate armies, most horses were used as **cavalry** mounts. Cavalry troops could swiftly ride through a battlefield to overwhelm enemies on the ground. Cavalry horses were also used for scouting and making quick raids into enemy territory. Non-cavalry horses were used for carrying messages and supplies, pulling war wagons, and carrying officers between battlefields.

Mules were sometimes used for similar tasks as horses. But they were generally used away from the battlefield. Mules often hauled heavy weapons in long mule trains. Strong, sure-footed mules were also used as pack animals to carry supplies over rough mountain and forest trails.

cavalry—soldiers who travel and fight on horseback

Cincinnati

Union General Ulysses S. Grant once said that his horse, Cincinnati, was the finest horse he had ever seen. Others admired the big, fast horse too. Someone once offered $10,000 in gold for Cincinnati. But Grant turned the offer down. When Grant became U.S. president in 1869, he brought Cincinnati with him to Washington, D.C.

WAR FACT

President Lincoln was one of only two people General Grant ever let ride on Cincinnati.

Winchester

On October 19, 1864, Union General Philip Sheridan received an urgent message near Winchester, Virginia. Some of his troops were under attack in Cedar Creek, 12 miles (19 kilometers) away. Sheridan jumped on his big Morgan horse, Rienzi, and sped off. Because of the horse's great speed, the general arrived in time to rally his troops and turn a near loss into a Union victory. To honor the horse's achievement, Sheridan renamed him Winchester. Today Winchester's preserved body can be seen in the Smithsonian American History Museum.

Little Sorrel

Little Sorrel belonged to Confederate General Thomas "Stonewall" Jackson. This strong, even-tempered horse wasn't afraid of gunfire. His courage was helpful for Jackson, who was not a great horseman. After Jackson was killed in 1863, Little Sorrel became a true celebrity. He made many public appearances until he died in 1886.

Traveller

Confederate General Robert E. Lee's horse, Traveller, was famous for his great intelligence, courage, and spirit. In the Battle of Spotsylvania, Traveller saved Lee's life by rearing up to avoid a cannonball that nearly hit them.

When Lee died in 1870, Traveller marched in his funeral procession. Today Traveller is buried in Lexington, Virginia, near Lee's own grave.

Limbers

The limber was a two-wheeled horse-drawn cart used for pulling support wagons and artillery guns. These carts carried a copper-covered **ammunition** chest. Wagons or artillery were attached to the rear of a limber by a hook.

limber

Caissons

caisson

Caissons were two-wheeled support wagons attached to limbers. They carried two backup chests of ammunition. Caissons also carried a spare wheel and limber pole strapped beneath the cart.

WAR FACT

Wagon trains were assembled in a particular order. Ammunition wagons usually came first, then troops and artillery. Forge and battery wagons brought up the rear. It took about 25 wagons to supply 1,000 soldiers.

Forge Wagons

A blacksmith forge wagon was set on two wheels and pulled by a limber. Forge wagons were used for shoeing horses, repairing weapons and equipment, and other metalworking jobs. Forge wagons carried a furnace, **bellows**, and coal to fuel the fires. They were sometimes known as battery forges.

Battery Wagons

These covered carts were also attached to limbers. They were longer than caissons or forge wagons and had a rounded roof. Battery wagons carried tools for making and repairing equipment such as carriages and saddles. They also held extra harnesses and parts for emergency repairs.

ammunition—bullets and other objects that can be fired from weapons

bellows—an air bag with two handles used to blow air into a fire

13

Ambulance Wagons

The earliest four-wheeled ambulance wagon was the Tripler. Like most ambulances of the time, it had a canvas roof and was pulled by four horses. The Tripler could carry six seated patients along with four others lying on beds. Some ambulances were "double-deckers" with two beds above and two more below. Most ambulances were equipped with stretchers, bandages, and medical tools such as surgical saws.

WAR FACT

The Union military assigned one ambulance wagon for every 150 troops in battle. Each group also got two medical supply wagons.

Sutler Wagons

Non-military sutler wagons were like stores on wheels. They sold supplies to soldiers such as paper, razors, and knives. They also offered soap, coffee, and tobacco. If soldiers were still hungry after eating their rations, they could also buy high-priced food from sutler wagons.

Media Wagons

Civil War reporters often visited battlefields in small horse-drawn wagons. But photographers had a harder time. Photography was a new technology at that time and cameras were big and heavy. Photographers also needed special chemicals and supplies that took up a lot of space. They often arrived after the battle in their own large, makeshift wagons.

Wagon Parks

Large wagon parks provided important services. Blacksmiths, carpenters, and other craftsmen worked in these parks. Horses and mules were re-shod and wagons were repaired. These parks serviced hundreds of wagons at once.

Locomotives

In the Civil War, train engines, or locomotives, could pull an average of 16 to 22 train cars. The most powerful engines could haul 50 loaded freight cars. Union trains averaged about 15 to 20 miles (24 to 32 km) per hour. Confederate trains moved more slowly at about 8 to 10 miles (13 to 16 km) per hour.

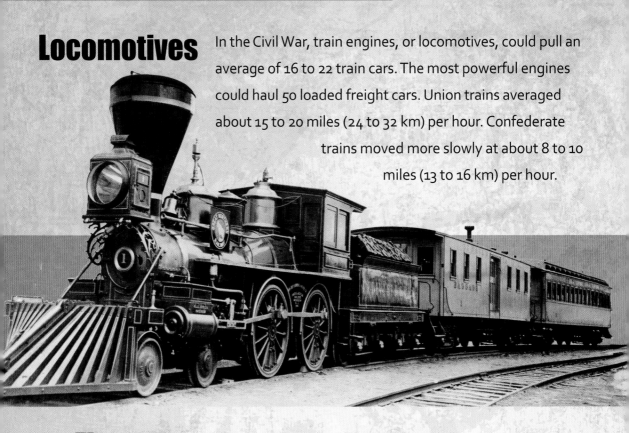

Flatcars

Flatcars were used for transporting heavy artillery and troops. They were usually pulled by train engines. But some were operated by soldiers manually. Sometimes artillery could be fired from a flatcar on the move. Flatcars usually had no walls or roofs. Soldiers sometimes fired weapons from behind iron shields that sloped inward at a 45-degree angle.

Artillery and Rifle Cars

Iron-plated artillery boxcars carried several cannons. Troops fired the cannons through hatches as the train rolled along. Armor on the first artillery cars was thin. It offered protection only from small-arms fire.

But later cars had thickly-armored, sloping sides that deflected heavy enemy fire.

Rifle cars were similar to artillery cars, but were fitted with interior armor instead of iron plates. These rail cars had small holes that allowed soldiers to fire small weapons such as handguns and muskets.

Passenger Cars

These cars were designed to carry up to 56 passengers. But during the war as many as 100 troops were crammed together in one car. Passenger cars were usually located between the train engine and flatcars. Being positioned next to flatcars filled with armed soldiers and heavy weapons offered greater protection from enemy attacks.

Ambulance Cars

Early in the war, sick and wounded soldiers were taken from the battlefield by any means available. But later, big boxcars were made into ambulance cars that held several patients. These specialized rail

cars included stretchers, sinks, tanks to hold fresh water, and kitchens to prepare hot meals. Sometimes groups of ambulance cars were hooked together to form a hospital train. These trains carried wounded soldiers to field hospitals for immediate care, and then to larger hospitals in distant cities.

Handcars

Handcars were small hand-powered vehicles that didn't call attention to themselves. A crew of four men operated the hand crank to make the vehicles move. Handcars were often used for inspecting rail lines. In some cases they carried cannons for surprise attacks. However, these missions were risky. Handcars could not travel as fast as trains. And they did not offer soldiers protection from enemy fire.

The Great Locomotive Chase

No Civil War locomotive is more famous than the *General*. On April 12, 1862, a group of Northerners **hijacked** the Confederate steam locomotive in Georgia. They planned to burn bridges and destroy tracks behind them as they headed north.

But the Confederates were soon in pursuit and the 87-mile (140-km) chase was on. The Southerners began on foot, switched to a handcar, and then chased the Northerners in three different locomotives. When they finally caught up, the *General* was out of steam and had stopped on the tracks. Out of 22 Northerners, eight managed to escape. The other 14 were caught and either hung or exchanged for Confederate prisoners.

WAR FACT

Steam locomotives were often sent alone to gather intelligence on the enemy. These train engines were also used to scout unfamiliar areas. Locomotives even served as rams to destroy enemy equipment.

hijack—to take control of a vehicle by force

Ch.3 >> Vehicles in the Water

At the start of the war, the Union had fewer than 50 available ships. The Confederacy had no navy at all. Eventually, both sides built a variety of warships. Most were steam-powered, but ships with sails were still common. Both sides also secretly created submarines to gain an advantage in the war.

Frigates

Frigates were similar to battleships but weren't as large. They were also less costly and easier to sail. At the start of the war, the Union Navy had five 54-gun frigates. It also had a number of smaller frigates with fewer guns.

Tinclads

Merchant steamers were often modified into "tinclads" during the war. These wooden boats were quickly and cheaply converted into combat vessels. Sheets of metal were installed around the sides of these boats. Then various types of artillery were mounted on their decks.

Ironclad Battleships

These big warships defended the East coast and patrolled on large rivers. They were built of wood and then fitted with iron armor. Ironclads commonly carried heavy guns such as cannons and **mortars**. Some were also equipped with gun **turrets**.

The *Virginia* vs. the *Monitor*

The first battle between two ironclad ships occurred on March 9, 1862, at Hampton Roads, Virginia. The Confederacy's ship was the CSS *Virginia*. The *Virginia* had been the USS *Merrimack*. But the South recovered it and converted it to an ironclad. The Union warship was the USS *Monitor*. The ships were fairly evenly matched. While the *Virginia* was bigger, the *Monitor* was faster and carried the heaviest weapons available. The battle ended with no clear winner.

mortar—a short cannon that fires shells into the air at a high angle

turret—a rotating, armored structure that holds a weapon on top of a military vehicle

Mortar Boats

Mortar boats were armored barges built for attacking forts from a river. River mortar boats were usually built on flatbed vessels that looked more like rafts than boats. Each boat was armed with a heavy 13-inch (33-cm) mortar placed on a wooden platform. A **bulwark** of tall wooden poles was built around the mortar for protection. By March 1862 the Union Navy had 30 of these boats operating with the Mississippi River Squadron.

Naval Rams

Naval rams were armored steam-powered ships with strong, pointed **prows**. These ships were used to ram into enemy ships to damage and sink them. Naval rams also carried several heavy guns for defense.

bulwark—a solid wall-like structure used for defense

prow—the pointed front part of a boat or ship that sits above the water

Tugboats

Before the war, tugboats were often used to haul loads taken off bigger vessels. But during the war, some were equipped with guns. The Union used them to fire on forts along rivers in Virginia, North Carolina, and Georgia. The small, steam-powered boats were easy to operate. But they could carry only light or medium-weight guns.

Transport Ships

At the start of the war, both the North and South had few ships to quickly transport troops and supplies. To get more transport ships, both sides often rented or bought private ships. Sometimes merchant ships were seized for the war effort as well. These ships were then equipped as wartime transports to carry troops, food, clothing, and other military supplies.

WAR FACT

The Union Navy used a new type of gunboat called a "double-ender." These gunboats easily moved through shallow water. But their biggest advantage was the ability to move backward or forward without having to turn around.

The *Intelligent Whale*

The Union Navy had little success with submarines. One experimental Union submarine, which was never used in battle, was the *Intelligent Whale*. It was 28-feet (8.5-m) long and carried up to 13 crew members. The *Whale* could stay underwater for up to 10 hours. It had no engine and required four people to turn a crank to power its propellers.

WAR FACT

One of the *Alligator*'s early missions was to blow up a railroad bridge over a Virginia river. But the river was too shallow. It was impossible for the *Alligator* to hide under the water.

The *Alligator*

The *Alligator* was launched in 1862. This green-painted sub was 47-feet (14-m) long and held a crew of 15 men. The *Alligator* was driven with oars at first. But they were later replaced with a propeller that doubled the submarine's speed. However, it was still slow and hard to handle. In April 1863 the *Alligator* sank during a violent storm near Charleston, South Carolina.

CSS *H.L. Hunley*

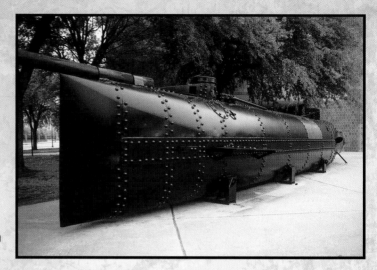

This 40-foot (12-meter) Confederate sub was built from an old train engine steam boiler. A crew of eight men worked together to turn a hand crank that drove the sub's propeller. The *Hunley* sank the Union ship USS *Housatonic* with a **spar torpedo** in 1864. It was the first sub to succeed in sinking an enemy target. Not long after sinking the *Housatonic*, the *Hunley* sank. Scientists think the sub may have been damaged during its attack on the *Housatonic*. In May 1995 divers found the *Hunley* underwater off the South Carolina coast. It was recovered in 2000.

CSS *David*

The CSS *David* was a Confederate submarine powered by steam. In October 1863 this sub attacked a Union ship off South Carolina's coast. The sub's 65-pound (29.5-kg) torpedo hit its mark, although the ship did not sink.

spar torpedo—an explosive device attached to a long pole used to destroy an enemy target

25

On June 18, 1861, Thaddeus S. C. Lowe floated above Washington, D.C., in a balloon called *Enterprise*. While in the air, he sent a message to President Lincoln with a **telegraph**. Lincoln was so impressed that he decided to create the Union Balloon Corps and put Lowe in charge.

By January 1862 the Union had several hydrogen-filled balloons. The balloons had crews of 30 to 50 men who transported, operated, and maintained them.

telegraph—a machine that uses electrical signals to send messages over long distances

The silk balloons were used for **reconnaissance** work to learn enemy troop movements. The balloons floated between 300 and 500 feet (91 and 152 m) in the air. From there the balloonists, called aeronauts, could safely watch enemy action from a distance. They would then use telegraphs to report enemy activities.

Union Balloons

Name	Passengers
Enterprise	1
Union	5
Intrepid	5
Constitution	3
United States	3
Washington	2
Eagle	1
Excelsior	1

Gas Wagons

Lowe also designed wagons that carried equipment for inflating balloons. These "inflating wagons" each carried a portable gas-making machine that followed the balloons during missions. Each balloon needed two of these wagons to be fully inflated.

reconnaissance—a mission to gather information about an enemy

The Union Balloon Corps created problems for the Confederates. Southern forces had to use sneaky methods to hide troop locations and movements from Union balloons. They kept their campfires hidden at night, pitched tents under trees, and even built fake cannons to try to fool the Balloon Corps.

The South soon began work on its own balloon service. At first the Confederates didn't have hydrogen gas to fill their balloons. The first Southern balloon was filled with hot air instead. But hot air was unreliable, and the fire needed to keep the air hot was dangerous.

Eventually, the South found ways to get hydrogen gas to fill their balloons. But Southern forces couldn't create the gas while on the move. Instead, they filled their balloons in the cities. The balloons were then towed by train or boat.

The South managed to get only two gas balloons into action. But one balloon did have some success. The *Gazelle*'s crew was able to see and report on Union troop movements in Virginia. The information gave the South the upper hand in the Seven Days Battle.

···IMPROVING THE ODDS···

The success of ironclad ships in the Civil War led to more advanced armored warships in later wars.

Compared to today's military vehicles, Civil War vehicles were crude and slow. But people kept trying to make more advanced war machines. Both sides used new vehicles to gain an advantage and improve their odds of winning the war.

Glossary

ammunition (am-yuh-NI-shuhn)—bullets and other objects that can be fired from weapons

artillery (ar-TIL-uh-ree)—cannons and other large guns used during battles

bellows (BELL-ohs)—an air bag with two handles used to blow air into a fire

bulwark (BUHL-wuhrk)—a solid wall-like structure used for defense

cavalry (KA-vuhl-ree)—soldiers who travel and fight on horseback

constitution (kahn-stuh-TOO-shuhn)—the system of laws that states the rights of the people and the powers of the government

hijack (HYE-jak)—to take control of a vehicle by force

mortar (MOR-tur)—a short cannon that fires shells into the air at a high angle

prow (PROW)—the front part of a boat or ship

reconnaissance (ree-KAH-nuh-suhnss)—a mission to gather information about an enemy

secede (si-SEED)—to formally withdraw from a group or an organization, often to form another organization

spar torpedo (SPAR tor-PEE-doh)—an explosive device attached to a long pole used to destroy an enemy target

telegraph (TEL-uh-graf)—a machine that uses electrical signals to send messages over long distances

turret (TUR-it)—a rotating, armored structure that holds a weapon on top of a military vehicle

Read More

Fein, Eric. *Weapons, Gear, and Uniforms of the Civil War.* Equipped for Battle. North Mankato, Minn.: Capstone Press, 2012.

Olson, Kay Melchisedech. *The Terrible, Awful, Civil War: The Disgusting Details about Life During America's Bloodiest War.* Disgusting History. North Mankato, Minn.: Capstone Press, 2010.

Stanchak, John. *Civil War.* DK Eyewitness Books. New York: DK Pub., 2011.

Internet Sites

FactHound offers a safe, fun way to find Internet sites related to this book. All of the sites on FactHound have been researched by our staff.

Here's all you do:

Visit *www.facthound.com*

Type in this code: 9781429699129

Super-cool stuff! Check out projects, games and lots more at **www.capstonekids.com**

Index